GRATITUDE IS COOL ATTITUDE

Rupi Panesar

authorHOUSE®

AuthorHouse™ UK
1663 Liberty Drive
Bloomington, IN 47403 USA
www.authorhouse.co.uk
Phone: UK TFN: 0800 0148641 (Toll Free inside the UK)
UK Local: (02) 0369 56322 (+44 20 3695 6322 from outside the UK)

Published by AuthorHouse 03/24/2022

ISBN: 978-1-6655-9737-1 (sc)
ISBN: 978-1-6655-9736-4 (e)

Print information available on the last page.

Any people depicted in stock imagery provided by Getty Images are models, and such images are being used for illustrative purposes only. Certain stock imagery © Getty Images.

Cover Creator: Aminah Adeyemi

This book is printed on acid-free paper.

Acknowledgments

What does the word Acknowledgement mean to you?

To me, personally, Acknowledgement means being thankful and appreciating everything and everyone around you. A heartfelt thank you to all that have been there for me through hardships and the good times. You know who you are. Sending nothing but peace and harmony into the universe for you all.

What is Gratitude?

Gratitude can be anything you want it to be and how you use it. Just remember to be thankful for what you want and what you have, and it will come to you in abundance. If you're thankful for what you have and if you practice the art of manifesting, you can achieve anything!

What is Cool Attitude?

Cool attitude can mean many things to you on a personal level. It could be you having awareness of your surroundings while keeping focused with what's going on around you. Or it could even just be the simple fact of being aware and composed to what you know what is right for you. It's important to stand strong as an individual. Just don't forget that being cool can also mean being humble and showing kindness.

Manifest.

Let your amazing thoughts become reality. Send good vibes into the universe and they'll come back to you.

I express great attitude for being a better person every day. Thinking and being strong will guide me to be the superior person I am.

Deep Breathing... 10, 9, 8, 7, 6, 5, 4, 3, 2, 1... Relax and breath

I am thankful for my positive thoughts which enable me to create positive feelings and emotions, such as feeling happy, achieving new goals, or even feeling peaceful.

I show immense gratitude to the Universe for having the perfect self-image. I know and believe I am perfect in every way, shape, and form. No one can tell me any different.

Deep Breathing... 10, 9, 8, 7, 6, 5, 4, 3, 2, 1... Relax and breath

I am thankful for believing and knowing that I am an amazing individual. I hold the patience to allow my dreams, aspirations, and goals to manifest.

I express great attitude for all the good days I have. Any bad days I have will manifest into amazing days where I achieve and succeed in anything I do.

Deep Breathing... 10, 9, 8, 7, 6, 5, 4, 3, 2, 1... Relax and breath

I am very thankful to have the courage and confidence
for allowing the universe to manifest my exceptional ideas,
options, and opinions.

I am so grateful for finding solutions to any problems and difficulties that come my way.

Deep Breathing... 10, 9, 8, 7, 6, 5, 4, 3, 2, 1... Relax and breath

I show admirable thankfulness for facing my fears and worries every day. I am so thankful for the strong and powerful thoughts that I can create in my mind to be a better individual.

I am profoundly grateful that I can and will reach new heights today and will not stop until I am satisfied with my own achievable goals.

Deep Breathing... 10, 9, 8, 7, 6, 5, 4, 3, 2, 1... Relax and breath

I am so thankful for being a positive and productive individual every day. The gratitude that I manifest will help me to grow.

I am so grateful for the patience that I practice and I know I will receive if I believe and show great kindness to everyone around me.

Deep Breathing... 10, 9, 8, 7, 6, 5, 4, 3, 2, 1... Relax and breath

The word Gratitude to me means being thankful for all the amazing and outstanding achievements that I have and will gain whilst learning the power of patience and courage.

I am forever grateful and thankful to the universe for all that I am and all that I will be in my foreseeable future.

Deep Breathing... 10, 9, 8, 7, 6, 5, 4, 3, 2, 1... Relax and breath·

I embrace immense gratitude for the strength to make the best choices today, that will guide me to achieve great decisions in all I do.

I am so grateful for believing that my positive thoughts and dreams will always come true. This will happen if I truly believe that my efforts will reap the benefits of my progression.

Deep Breathing... 10, 9, 8, 7, 6, 5, 4, 3, 2, 1... Relax and breath

I am grateful for all that I have. I am grateful for the food that I receive, the nourishment that keeps my body strong and healthy for the day ahead.

I show great gratitude for the mind and power to believe in my abilities and beyond. I know that in my heart, my gratitude will show me the right path to continue with my ambitions and goals.

Deep Breathing... 10, 9, 8, 7, 6, 5, 4, 3, 2, 1... Relax and breath

I show great kindness to the universe for allowing me to pick myself up and try again if I feel like I have fallen. But the universe will not fail me, it will help me to grow.

My gratitude shows me the way to be the best me, in every aspect of my life. Being kind and humble, helping others and respectful will guide me the way.

Deep Breathing... 10, 9, 8, 7, 6, 5, 4, 3, 2, 1... Relax and breath

My emotions may take over my gratitude at times, but I am forever thankful to all the support I have around me.

When I show full gratitude, I achieve more of what I want and desire. This will enable me to reach new heights to my full potential.

Deep Breathing... 10, 9, 8, 7, 6, 5, 4, 3, 2, 1... Relax and breath

I am forever thankful to the universe for accepting my strength and my personal goals that I know and will achieve.

I show great attitude towards my gratitude for all the exceptional actions I take every day. I show heartfelt gratitude for all that surround me and show me guidance.

Deep Breath... 10, 9, 8, 7, 6, 5, 4, 3, 2, 1... Relax

I am grateful for the patience within me, that will guide me to be the best that I can be.

I know, therefore I am a smart, clever and confident individual who will make my ambitions and dreams become a reality.

About me

Me, I'm just a humble and noble human being, trying to make a change for the generation and foreseeable future for all. Sounds funny and crazy if you're reading this, but just believe in yourself and work hard, talk about your amazing ideas, creations and positive thoughts without any boundaries, see where the world will take you. It is important to stay true to yourself and never forget who you are.

As they say... The world is your oyster.

Don't forget to just Breathe...

Printed in the United States
by Baker & Taylor Publisher Services